PIRATE PAUL
Makes a Booty Call

www.castlepointbooks.com

The Castle Point Books trademark is owned by Castle Point Publications, LLC.
Castle Point books are published and distributed by St. Martin's Publishing Group.

Illustrations by Chiara Galletti

ISBN 978-1-250-28526-3 (hardcover)
ISBN 978-1-250-28527-0 (ebook)

Our books may be purchased in bulk for promotional, educational, or business use.
Please contact your local bookseller or the Macmillan Corporate and
Premium Sales Department at 1-800-221-7945, extension 5442,
or by e-mail at MacmillanSpecialMarkets@macmillan.com.

First Edition: February 2023

10 9 8 7 6 5 4 3 2 1

PIRATE PAUL
Makes a Booty Call

Peggy Plank

illustrated by
Chiara Galletti

CASTLE POINT BOOKS
NEW YORK

On a faraway island
full of coconut trees
lived a swashbuckling pirate
and his parrot, Louise.

From the time his ship sank,
and he was clearly marooned,
Paul started his search for
a chest of doubloons.

You'd think he'd be lonely
living all by himself,
but he found isolation
to be great for his health.

He got into yoga,
and gardening, too.
He practiced his golf swing,
and whittled a shoe.

He took nice, long walks
on the beach all alone.
He learned how to knit,
and he baked a mean scone.

But pretty soon, even
those things were a bore.
And he started to wonder—
Blimey! Could there be more?

He dismissed the thought quickly,
and ventured to dream
of bountiful treasure—
What a glorious scene!

If I can find booty,
said the thought in his head,
I'll never be lonely.
I'll be rich instead!

Paul left on a mission
when the sun was a-scorchin'.
He trekked through the island
in search of a fortune.

It was when he returned
with no riches in hand,
that he noticed a clipper
pulling up to the sand.

Its crew disembarked
with smiles on their faces.
They'd been sailing in search
of this island for ages!

Paul drew his long sword,
and it gleamed in the sun.
"Step closer," he growled,
"and I'll reach for my gun."

A red-headed lassie
pushed past all the guys,
and despite the harsh warning,
looked him straight in the eyes.

She showed him a map
where an X marked the spot
of bountiful booty
they hadn't yet got.

"You know this place best,"
she said, "Join our search.
We can work as a team
and increase our net worth!"

"This is my island!"
he boasted with pride,
"So take all your mates,
and be gone with the tide!"

Though he talked a big game,
and he tried to pretend,
it was clear that inside,
Paul longed for a friend.

That night Paul snuck out,
with the map that he stole
and discovered a chest
full of gems and pure gold!

He should have been giddy
to have found all the treasure,
but, alas, there he sat
feeling no hint of pleasure.

He swallowed his feelings
and went back to his plan,
but that big trunk of booty
was too much for one man.

And although sunset yoga
had strengthened his core,
He threw out his back
trying to get it to shore.

Paul knew what to do—
he was no longer torn.
He gathered his breath,
and reached for his horn.

He sounded a call,
as he felt it his duty,
and the pirates came running,
knowing he'd found the booty.

Thanks to Paul's booty call,
they were richer than ever,
so they made him their captain,
and set sail together.

With gold in his chest
and joy in his heart,
one lonely old pirate
made a friendly new start.

So listen, ye mateys
seeking fortune and fame...

...when ye find ye some booty
remember Pirate Paul's name.